Into the bend of the river as far as we can go

John Mayer

ISBN 978-1-387-23628-2

First printing, September 2017

Copyright 2017 by John Mayer. All rights reserved. No part of this book may be reproduced in any form without the written consent of the author.

Written by John Mayer

Edited and cover design by Johanna Neuschwander

Image by John Mayer of Columbia River at Rooster Rock State Park

Introduction

I remember feeling wise and strong when I was the most broken. 'We can survive anything.' 'We do hard things.' 'Love is everything.' It's as if at the bottom of the human well there is a trampoline to bounce back towards the surface with. But it's only if you're all the way at the bottom that you can use it. And it will never get you all the way to the top again. Instead it is there like a guard against falling through. If you bounce just right, you might be able to propel from the deepest of depths half way up but there is a large wall to climb still. Anywhere but the bottom of the hole is full of slime and frustration; a slippery rock that used to feel like a foothold or a ledge just too small for fingertips to grasp. It's the hardest of work once you are ready to climb. The trampoline's springs made sure I didn't fall through the earth but now it's up to me to figure out the rest of the climb.

Ten months before I wrote the paragraph above, my child died in my wife's arms. We knew she would die before she was born because at 21 weeks of pregnancy, we learned that the hemispheres of her brain would have no bridge. There would be untellable--except to be undeniably massive-- impacts on her ability to live a life. My wife and I were devastated and struggled to know what was a right way forward. After countless doctors, endless prayers to gods we didn't know, and a soul searching that took us to a place inside neither of us knew existed, we decided. If our baby's life would be one of suffering, our role as parents would be to take the suffering away. It strikes me now, but didn't then, that this is what every parent wishes they could do when they see pain in their child. In this way we were lucky. We asked to say goodbye with compassion.

At 24 weeks, my wife was induced into labor and on September 27, 2017, our baby River was born. She lived with us for 90 minutes or so and we held her for a few hours longer. We kissed and studied her every part like any new parent does. In that time, we sang her lullabies and read her poetry, we showed her still-closed eyes pictures of her family and we told her how much she was loved. It was the most beautiful, the most profound, and the saddest thing I have ever been a part of.

The poems that follow were written in the months that followed. It helped me to write them. Collecting them from my journals and scraps of paper and ill-organized computer files was a way for me to start to climb out of the deepest grief I hope I will ever know. I humbly share them with whomever may find something for themselves; some toehold that might help as they climb their own wall of grief. If you know that person and are reading these words, give this book away. If you need another copy, I would like to give it to you.

We cannot protect each other from grief. Death will happen for all of us. If we love, grief will too. I hope that in sharing River's life and death there may be something good. She has made me a better person and while you will never get to meet her, I hope she can be part of your world, even for a moment.

> John Mayer

September

Navigation
8 days before

You will be about a pound
and translucent.

I will be able
to hold you as long as I need;
but how will I put you down?

The weight of that is already in my bones.

I learned tonight that you might breathe
and now, again, do not know what to wish for.
Death is not always the worst of it.

So many times, this week and last,
I have wished for religion.
I imagine there are answers there.

Your mother is strong.
She will bring you from there
to here and beyond.
She knows how to pack for such a journey
even though we don't know
where we are going.

You are one in a trillion,
a star hidden in the shadow.
We will always know where to look
when we can look up and out again.
You've already shown us the way.

Two views
4 days before

There is a piece missing,
a hole where a bridge once stood.

It comes in fragments,
but I want the whole story.

The River looks still from above—
omnipresent and eternal.
Each drop has come from a place
and has somewhere else to be
but each drop is here now,
singular.

I will stand in our reflections
and stare back up at the surface
while you make your way
through us to the other side.

But the whole of
this is yet to be.
Only I imagine I can see
it from here and already
wish it could be otherwise.

Tomorrow
2 days before

We go in tomorrow.
Momma will give birth.
We will say goodbye.
We've begun this work already.
I feel numb.
Packed, but wholly unprepared.
It will be so hard on her.
How do I do this
But one step at a time?
I have to be strong.
Or at least I have to be.

This is love
1 day before & 7 days after

Time is moving outside of itself today. I imagine you still in there, dark and with the comfort of warm. Out here, fall exhales the last breaths of summer and we wait. This is love.

A fountain mimics your name, River, rambling up the glass and brick of the hospital walls. I wish I could hear your voice instead. Instead, I will sing to the stars and listen for the echo in the chasm between. This is love.

You will fit in the palm of my hand and your ashes will fill a thimble. You are tiny, but infinite. You will overflow us with wonder and grief—just two other words for love.

Our imagined future never looked like this. We thought we had time, but now the corners don't line up. The horizon has been folded so the sky and earth don't meet at the edge anymore. We've been tilted sideways by your coming and your going. This is love.

River, you have swollen your momma with your waters. She has grown you with strength and determination. You have sipped the food from our garden for 23 weeks. But this world out here is no good for you. Untethered, now, we say goodbye. This is love.

Your tiny body held in hands learning a new tender. Your body cradled by yellow soft wool knit with generations of tears. We marveled at your fingers and kissed your toes, held you on our chests where the weight of you is etched. We read you this poem and sang you a song. This is love like I've never known.

Our garden now is full with you now. With muscles driven by love, clutter is cleared and a cradle carved to hold our bodies when they are too heavy to be upright. Each pebble placed and each weed removed with you in my bones. The anemone blooms in fall and knows how to turn to the sun. This is love.

We dance to loud music across an old wood floor and know you are in the drums. This is love.

The first day without
1 days after

The only part that felt real was holding you.
Now it's your momma's hands that feel most empty.
One pound and three ounces never weighed so heavily.
Eleven and a half inches unfurled, but you were mostly curled,
holding yourself close.
Your long fingers felt like feathers, but this was not flight.
Your momma sang you to sleep after an hour of breath we
shared.

> *I love you in the morning—and in the afternoon—*
> *I love you in the evening and underneath the moon.*

Tucked into knit yellow blanket, loved already, you made it full.
Your head was soft and smelled like seagrass and blood; it fit
perfectly in my palm.
Your elbows and knees sharp like your parents'. Your toes long
like your momma's.
Your veins mosaicked a watershed across your body.
They told us you could recognize our voices, our vibrations,
so we read you poems
        and hummed
                and cried.

Your heart stopped but we kept singing.
The only part that felt real was holding you.
There are no metaphors yet.

October

At the edge
7 days after

We walk through willows
that smell like Alaskan highland.
On the other side is sand
that smells like the sea, 100 miles west.
The Columbia spans in front of us
Oregon's cliffs rise behind,
ancient and in motion.

This expanse is beautiful and barren.
We have never touched it until now,
until you.

You bring us down and out
as far into the bend of the river as we can go.
We stand like two wrongly planted trees and
look out into the wind.

It begins to rain.
Big fat fall raindrops meant to melt ambition
and wash away summer.
These drops are too heavy for clouds
and beg to find the river.
They fall down and push east across
the surface with the help of wind.
You have been swirling here.
They bathe us while we watch the water
flow west to the ocean.
Now damp and here with you,
We can laugh and run our way back.

We have kissed and breathed and touched you.
We can return.

Running
9 days after

Running in the rain, I felt a poem arise.
And fade.
And rise.
And fade.
It was like breath.
It was like you.
Your facts are finite.
Your imprint, infinite.
No longer is there any value in the time of things,
But only in their depth.
The idea arrived,
Then left with the next step.
A drop in an overflowing bucket,
Released to the river
And home again…

Our garden is filled with you
12 days after

Our garden is filled with you
and fifty friends' tears.
They watered your flowers
yesterday with word of your going.
It was nice to see them cry too.
We have cried so much my face feels
more strange when it's dry.

I hugged giants for minutes at a time
and felt miniscule in the scheme of things.
The words. Poetry. Filled that blue air.
"I love your precious heart,"
they sang in lullaby
and spoke of River and irises,
water and work.
Deep in the eyes
that met mine
I saw them moving
to the deaths they've known.
In the middle of the web,
we were wrapped and held
in grief shared across lives.
She brought us there.
A gift.

Tuesday
Two's day
Too day
Today
14 days after

It's been two weeks today,
Tuesday.
When I crossed the Willamette today,
a thousand crows spiraled off
the Westside skyscrapers
and silhouetted themselves against
the purple pink under lit clouds.
I heard their caws through the sunroof and imagined you
somehow in the chaos,
exploded.

Today family climbs on planes east,
across a country's web of rivers,
to land with hands held out.
A reach back west. Maybe we
can touch waters where we are and
know eventually they run together
out there.

I think of your body. It is returning.
Today--tomorrow--already--ashes.
But always also in my skin and bones.
You will be burnt again when I die.
And before, we will crawl back to the banks of the river
and sit in the mud. Together.

Fall flowers
16 days after

I've been walking slowly this week.
There isn't much that seems worth rushing for.
The water poured over its banks before
and we are standing in the rain,
wet already.
The drops that are falling on you
hit the petals first
their faces shake to life
with purpose and invitation.
They do not hunker or hide.
They do not give in.
They open the tears they're given
like a gift and accept.

The drops map
origin and history,
continents and the inconceivable
before they land here in your garden.
Flower says, "Thank you,"
straightens her back and looks up again.

Mouth of the Columbia
19 days after

We went to where all the water goes,
where the rain and river release—
and all I could think about was you
slipping past and returning.
The salmon teach lessons about that.
So do the tides, a twice daily exhalation
of silt for salt; an exchange of chemistry.
Expectation shifting too.
A new balance.

My vision grows dark under a stormy sky
only flashes of lightning punctuated
the waves blowing inland from Japan.
They do not have the order and grammar
of the regular return of tides.
These roll and slam at askew angles.
Their sounds are chaotic and present.

And yet, what I see in the storm is nothing to be afraid of—
there is nothing left to be afraid of
but staying down at the bottom, where the
water is thrown and mixed new
for too long.
In there, you can drown.

We aren't meant to stay there forever.
But it's important to dive under and see.
I wonder if it will settle to a rhythm,
not a whirlpool's grasp pulling me under
but one that I can surf.
So far I only feel struck.

A haiku
24 days after

River, you are still.
Vast and particular.
I feel it all now.

Water
27 days after

In a drop, you separate.
A thousand pieces each
whole in and of itself.
An eternity of salt and
silt, of tears and vapors,
is in each of the
many drops I run towards.
Together a million make a
puddle waiting for a million
more to join, to push past
the inertia of company
and make motion to the drain,
      rediscover physics:
a creek, a run, a wash.
Water always moves down, able to
find a path without a map:
gravity's cartographer.
It works until
the fill is too much for the container.
A creek will rise and breach.
Banks of root and mud will give.
The river will eddy back on itself,
before circling towards
eventuality.
That is where I find myself:
at the confluence of
continuity and chaos—it
looks like water can
run backwards from here.

Four weeks
28 days after

Four weeks ago was your birthday
but I can't kiss you this morning.
The wind is cold and chaotic but
all I feel is you in my chest.
For weeks, you are all I see
behind my eyelids
or in the clouds
or tea or rain
or the river with each bridge
that I cross.

You are there: River.
For this week I try to
learn from you, with
you by my side.

But you fill my ears with
white. I can't hear the
words for syllables
for days.
This is not for the weak.

In the wind
32 days after

It's here where life is.
Where the weight lifts
and presence alone is magic.

Breathing the exhalations of
the shedding leaves and their trees
my gratitude unnoticed or ignored
the other three thousand times through
these trails. Their breath is soft.
It is enough to make me smile,
weightless and meant for exactly
the person who passes.

Silence is hard to find, but I can
talk to you in the quiet:
when the white noise of wind
drowns out
the distractions and the rhythm
of left-foot, right-foot, left-foot
that sets a metronome
grounded in a body's response to the moment,
I can hear you.

There is something gigantic about
Being connected to the universe.
But gravity does that for all of us.
The trees just refuse to let that dictate the paths of their trunks.
They may bow with the weight of the rain,
but breath has them growing against the physics of time.
And there, in the moment it had to happen,
with my left toes arching off the ground,
ready to trust my right leg to catch the weight,
I saw her in the breeze, between the trees.
Not so much a vision but her negative
and I was lost.
Both fully present in the moment and nowhere at all.

Marcelle's altar
33 days after

You are on altars
of people who love
you but will never see you.
Their hearts swell because
you have shown them something
new; something familiar.
You are on the tongues of poets.
We have known them over years that,
when counted against your weight
in this world, seem inconsequential.
They write lines for you, now,
sometimes like for the first time.
You are in the water that makes fog
hang between hills.
You are the water in the soil,
next year's roots feeding slowly in October.
You are both the mist
falling off the mountain's ledge and
the droplet that echoes back off the
surface of the water below.
So small, but making
time stop.

November

The shape of a soul
44 days after

It is the shape of an egg
and orange, each time I've
seen it. Seen in heat and
at the deepest point of silence
I can feel it in my hands.
I hold it delicately at first.
Reaching through the semi-solid
of my abdomen pushing
guts aside, the first time
I touched it, electricity came
easily. I was reaching to my elbow
through Jello. I could hold
the egg and be warmed.
The second time was the same.
I could come and go, dipping
my hands toward electricity
and feeling something like grace,
like truth, the place where truth
lives. If that's the place I'm
so glad to know it's there. Because
the third time it was
harder to find. The hole
had to be bigger. Like digging
through wet sand, and quickly
before the hole filled in.
But when I did, it was a careful
excavation.

Faith
47 days after

There is a full moon up there.
My loved ones on the other side
of the country or of life
have reported that it's beautiful.
I can see it in my mind too,
I looked for it last night
but the clouds are thick here
and heavy like our tears.

How do we know it's there?
By faith like that in gravity
It pulls rain down from the sky
    By reading and by rhythm
      by their going and us knowing.

It is the other kind of
knowing that lives between
the moons. The kind that
is not in the folds of books.

It feels like faith but I've
rarely known the word.
Now it says the moon is up there
full and bright and whole
when all I see is rain drops from
a slated sky.

Bow my head.
One foot falls on the gravel.
It should be enough to start
a faith that another step will follow.
Is how it's always been.

And so the moon will always be
even in November's clouds.

**Japanese gardens
(A walking meditation)**
48 days after

There's a place where the still
seeming water has collected all the
leaves that once hung from the skeletons above.
People collect like that too.
Going to where motion
has landed them.
There is the edge, where stillness
is possible, where drifters push from.
The sign tells me there's only
One Way. It seems out of place
in a garden where gravity and time
have been guides for so long. The
water didn't need a sign to find its way down.
One camellia still has blooms.
It is dropping its pink layers slowly—
like weeks of tears unswept. Its colors
offer contrast to the greens and greys that
fall has left behind otherwise.
It's the first day I can see my breath
or the first time it's caught my attention.
We nod at each other.

Jazz station meditation
49 days after

Let the flute lift you
right through the top of your head.
Listen close for the high tones.
Let them land and pull.. Let them
fill and keep lifting eyelids that would
rather close it all off today.

There is light etching orange
on the edge of purple clouds
at sunrise.
Before the rain comes back today,
look up. Know there is a sun
on the other side.
Lean on the earth's rotation
to mean something today.
Sometimes it's all you need.
Sometimes it's all you have.

Piano refills the radio and I
tune back in. Here
my heart is racing and I have to catch my breath.
pace myself.

 Rubber-banding
back to this here, this now.
Music lets joy and
the shadowed sunlight into these lines.

A River haiku
50 days after

You call it Sister.
I cry her name at the thought
That every river is.

A dream
56 days after

"*Blackbirds singing in the dead of night…*"
like the dreams that wake me sweating.
"*Into the light of a dark black night…*"
like when your eyes open to mine.
They are blue-grey. The color
of dry river rocks.
I see the impossible smile on your lips,
pursed like you already know that love is.
And I forget, just for a minute, that
I'll be lonely without you. Your whole body
hugs my wrist.
I rest the other on your back.
All thirty-two vertebrae imprint on
my palm like pebbles under my skin;
I can still feel them there.
Against reason, I see your face
turn up to mine. Your closed eyes
open and blink at me. They aren't supposed
to open but they stare.
I feel a breath pull into tiny lungs
mostly filled, and your eyes close again.
As your breath pushes out, I hear a whisper of,
"loved." So it's okay.

Two months
61 days after

Yesterday was two months
and we cried, River.
A quilt arrived in the mail.
It was meant for two months
from now, in January.
Now it remembers who
you were in September.
Today your sister remembered.
You entered her game
And I wish it weren't this way:

"I got this sister, River
and she went away.
You be sister and don't go away…"
"Okay," I say, wishing it all could be
untrued.

December

At Stephen's beach
Christmas 2016
88 days after

Everybody I see is with somebody else.
What none of them can see is that
I am too.
I smile and nod grimly
to their wishes of a merry day.
Perhaps they can see the futility
of their wishes;
they all have pity in their eyes
while I wear grief on my sleeves.
I keep walking the miles of sand
one step at a time with my attention
on my…
Let wind come in
Inhale.
Let rain blow out.
Exhale.
With each breath and in each step
I know the presence of my brother
     of my daughter
          and am lightened.
My shoulders fall back away from my ears
jaw unclenches and my eyes are allowed to
open and see.

It is like waking from a dream to feel you here.
All six foot two of you—all eighteen ounces of you—
is there in the meeting of the wind and the waves,
where spray pushes backwards against a forward moving wall.
You are in salt feeding moss holding tight to green hillsides
before being tipped into the sea in next year's storm.
You are in the hundred-year-old driftwood gripping
to a life it left thousands of miles away where half
of a shared memory has been taken beyond our reach.
You are in etchings in the sand painted in a wave's decline.

The rivulets look like roots
or veins.
There is life there,
fragile, but full of grace.
Temporary, like all of us.
The clouds change again and blow the two of you back to sea.
I am back on your beach full of sand where the wind shifts particles
without attention, but with great purpose. I breathe your salt in and exhale.

Three months
90 days after

It's been three months
and my heart gives out.
       It's only been three months...
One season, an equinox to a solstice.
The whole time, it's been getting darker.
The day before yesterday I know as the day
I learned magic. It was Christmas.
And the beach turned white when
I thought of you.
It melted moments later in the sun
and I was left with rivulets of
water's return through sand
and a photograph.
But really, what is left is belief:
with the right attention
and in the right place
you can be with the dead.
I wonder if the place actually matters.
I wonder if it's death that matters.
I think, actually, it is only the love that matters.

January

In a week
110 days after

In a week, you were going to be born.

If you were still there, I imagine your struggle for life, for breath, for freedom to and freedom from. I imagine your face: unsure of where or what but sure all was wrong. I imagine the chaos of emergency, all sharp tones and automation, the rushed pace and fervor of a rescue. I imagine seeing your eyes open, suddenly wide, all pupils and terror. I imagine crying with your momma and trying to understand our choices from here; from this birth that never happened.

In a week, you were going to be born.

You are not still here because we made a choice. Sixteen weeks ago, your momma pushed you into the world, into the hands of love. Even the doctors mourned your brevity. We all cried and kissed your too-small body. We watched a dozen or two or three small breaths pass until your heart stopped. Your momma was singing you a lullaby and your daddy kissed the back of your head. You could not feel pain yet. You never would.

In a week, you were going to be born.

But 20 weeks ago, when you were 20 weeks real, we found out. You had ten perfect, long fingers and toes. Your two eyes would be big like your momma's and your two arms would be ready to uncurl into the welcome of a world not meant for you. On the other side of perfection, the doctors saw what you lacked; a hole in your brain where a bridge should be. Our hearts broken by the negative space.

In a week, you were going to be born.

I am so glad that you will not. You will not face the pain of an unbridged brain. The doctors will not rush to save you with tubes and sterile instruments dropped into palms working to rescue an impossibility. Instead you already were born. Sixteen weeks ago, your momma pushed your peaceful too-small body into the quiet room. There we could love you with poetry and family's hands. There were generations waiting at the veil's edge with you. We were allowed to say goodbye.

In a week, you were going to be born.

Instead, on a day in late September I held your birth and death in the same breath. We did what every parent dreams of—take their child's pain away. We washed you in tears and wrapped you in arms made more tender than we'd known possible. Your whole life was ninety minutes. Your whole life was love.

Due date haikus
117 days after

I miss meeting you.
Today I should have kissed you.
I kiss wind instead.

Born too early to
know Winter's coat. I see you as
bare trees dance with wind.

The ferries took it.
Ferried to the other side
Where the dead keep us

As we keep the dead.
We can't see the border anymore
just like we can't see the moment
that the balloon disappeared.

Wind, filled with you, breaks
all the walls between our worlds.
"The veil is thinner than you think,"
I hear you whisper.

Always in love
124 days after

I'm in love,
I always will be.
Two marks on my arm,
two daughters born.
I will always love
but one will grow
and one will stay
here in memory,
curled and translucent.
She is little and beautiful.
The other keeps changing and
now I see her missing you
when I look into her eyes—all joy
but for the missing—knowing she is
but can't be a big sister. She will never meet
her little, but in dreams.
How do you do that when you are two?

February

Everything I touch
135 days after

Today's rain falls in fractals.
From clouds so small
they couldn't block the
whole of the sun.
The falling flares catch
the southern afternoon light,
bring attention to now—
and here.
They are a welcome reminder of duality:
the necessity of sun and the rain
the light and the dark of it all.
I know you can't come back.
I know you are always here.
I know you will never feel my touch.
I know you are in everything I touch.

Instead
144 days after

Today I wrote a poem instead.
I put the flour and the water and the yeast
from our kitchen's air together
and wrote this poem.
In a few days our kitchen
will smell like that life
when heat gives it back to the air.
Then we will eat the bread and know
If the poem was worth it in the end.

Fog
150 days after

Fog this thick
keeps futures close by.
There is a gift in now.
There was a gift in your moment.
A tree top in the distance
the only confirmation
of over there.
Here is where I feel you.
Here is where I can smile,
for a moment. Here you are,
in the stillness of a fog.

March

Morning sun
158 days after

At 7 am, the sun makes shadows in March
that catch like fall's light.
When you haven't
seen the sun in weeks, to feel it rise
and cast shadows on walls otherwise darkened
by winter,
it is like being brought back into now.
Here growth has needed both
the hibernation and the light,
the winter and the spring.
I am similar,
the hibernation has gotten me here.
Now it is time to wake up and see
how the world wants me now
and how do I want the world?

Searching
160 days after

I went looking for you in my breath this morning.
In the coolness of the air under my lip,
I thought I had you.
You blew away, inside—around—and out.
I kept searching.
Your sister says, "I love you,"
in an early-morning-crackled-voice,
like one you'd hear on an old radio
when the dial is just off the signal.
If I nudge the dial to the left or right,
maybe your voice
is in the in-between.
I can see you if I close my eyes.
I see the way you were at sunset—
tiny and mighty. Soft and supreme.
I see the way you are now—
in the stars and the wind.
I see the way I hope you will be—
making the universe glow.
But I still cannot hear you in the whispers
like I wish I could.

Full moon
165 days after

There is a full moon tonight
and tomorrow is my birthday.
I like when I find synchronicity
in the patterns cycles numbers.
There is comfort in the tiny coincidences
of finding a full moon rising in the east
huge and low, there is a pen close by
and my birthday is tomorrow.
The sounds in the otherwise dark
are of a city in the distance
but all I see is quiet.
I wish I could see your ghost tonight:
you would make noise in the dead leaves
and walk towards me. You were born
six months ago, but I see you as six years of girl.
All skinned knees and missing teeth—only here
in the garden, under a full moon, you wear white
like you never would have if you lived.
The moon is higher now,
trees like skeletons,
just now finding their bodies again.
It shines through frail clouds
and lights up the stars straight above.
Somewhere between here and there
is you. I'll go inside now, it is cold in the dark—
but you are a reminder to sit under stars in short sleeves
and look up.

April

Focus
185 days after

*A ghost I made you be
I only wanted us to be free.*

I'd rather sit
in the sun than
be any other way.

I'd forgotten the sound
of bee's wings
until I did just that.

Now I close my eyes
and feel warm
as if for the first time.

Chimes and train whistles
are in the distance.
I listen for the bee.

You are there in the echo.
You are there for me
to catch with my other ear.

A lecture
189 days after

Grief explodes your identity.
It starts time new.
It's that club you never wanted to join
       but needs your membership now.
The galaxy is too much to take in all at once. It's a screaming
stream of light and beauty, noise of music and chaos.
And grief's work
narrows the lens and tunnels the vision.
The firsts all begin again.
Death, after all, proves everything:
Control is slippery.
Time is rubber.
Memory is as real as the floor.
Regret connects the past to a future.
Conversations with the dead take a different sort of listening.

And now, you say, we're supposed to
stare into the galaxy of exploded stars
and find patterns again?
One day.

A new wave
192 days after

A new wave hit today.
She could be alive now.
I held her once.
I loved her since before.
I love her now.
It is in the mixing of tenses
that I find both a knowing
and a wish.

I should be whispering into ears,
Not the invisible space between.
I should be touching, not remembering,
the thinness of her skin.
She was warm and wet and fragile;
Aren't we all so.

Now it's been some months--
enough that laughter is possible
and not-crying is too.
Long enough now
that tears feel good again,
like a visitation that wracks
the body.
So I long for it. I long for you.

Omnipresent
195 days after

My friend wrote of icemelt
from the top of a mountain
and I think of you.
> A drop of omnipresence
> and mobility.
> Motion is the expectation,
> so change is the constant.

Where are you but here and under?
You are in and of every landscape
of melting snow and ice.
You are in each fern's tip
and in the pools at the roots,
the ones we can't see without digging.
You are a different kind of spring,
at once incredible and regrettable.

Need a little help
197 days after

It's been difficult lately:
the spring blooms and the way
the clouds move in and out in April
the way sunshine breaks the days into fractions now
and reminds other people about happiness and futures.
In our house we see what should've been more than a little.
It's like we are visiting the invisible and can feel the weight of
her presence and her absence at the same time.
It's like the weight of it all has doubled.
Maybe it's that gravity has quadrupled and the size of the world
has shrunk.
Deep breaths don't seem to stick for as long.
Or maybe it's that they don't sink as deeply into lungs hungry for
a reminder, or just hungry.
It's early in the day to feel so heavy.
I'm hoping the clouds will lift me with them
as the sun rises.

A day of signs
201 days after

A hawk crossed my path this afternoon,
I waved and smiled as Stephen flew over.
My brother always knows when I need him.
An old friend's Virginia accent crackled through the telephone as
I sat on a bench on 33rd and thought about faith.

My brother's friend is breaking, I learned.
Like Stephen did years before?
I was just teaching 2nd graders how to spell,
"friend will be with you until the e-n-d" this morning.

The only saint I'd follow sent me a text tonight.
It asked me to come to the old church.
She never calls on Monday, so I got my coat to go.

Opening the door to leave, Jesus was there.
"Do you need praying?" she asked
"Yes." "May we now?" "Yes"
"Are you Christian?"
"No, just taking good where we can find it."

I walked to the church to see this saint.
She showed me the floors we sanded upstairs
and asked me to serve.
I asked her for advice instead.
She said, "It's easy to give that, in fact,
I've already shown you."

I came home wondering
what it was I was shown
and there was my daughter,
remembering
the sister that died,
the one we couldn't see,
the one she named and cries for
just like we wail for our dead.

55

"I'm really sad about my sister
that died. She is still here though.
I love you daddy."
I think we've been chasing each other
like a game of hide and seek where
we each are seeking so well
we end up hiding.

Maybe, then, it is time
to sit still, to slow down
to pour the wine down to the roots
of the garden
and drink water instead.
The rains tell me so.

If I wait here without seeking,
if I sit without hiding,
you will be found.
In you, there is the part
that makes me whole again.

I'll sit then and serve,
a little chipped and broken
but I can wait and breathe. Let rising happen
against the rain.

Holding death again
208 days after

I held death again this morning.
A blue streak burst open against the grass, all wings and motion.
She turned her body sideways to the ground with one wing
        pointing straight to the sky
and veered into the path of my windshield.
Beauty smashed with ugly.
The blue jay and the Subaru.
Nature in the city when the city pirated the trees.
I felt it before I heard it. I wished
for death. I wanted ease and simplicity.
I wanted definition and an end.
With tremors in my hands, I bent to meet the bird.
She breathed through broken lungs and opened
an eye wide to her death.
So am I. Open.
I scoop her from the pavement and she flaps only once.
Quickly against my forearm, her wing relaxes. She sucks for
breath again. A little goes in. More comes out.
Death was there and I knew it. In that breath
she closed off, dropped away.
I looked to see if anybody else saw
it come. Nobody looked back
but the man asking for change on the opposite corner. He
        dropped his head.

Out there
210 days after

Breathe in the good.
Sweat out the bad.
Breath in the good.
Sweat out the bad.
Let the heat and the
water and the body
be tumbled together
like a tide changing
direction. The water pulling
the wind back to sea.

Let it go back
Be buoyed by salt.
Let's float together now
Because bout there far enough
Beyond the breakers
And miles from the River's edge
There is calm. I'll be there soon.

Permeability
212 days after

Definition:
The degree of magnetism of an object
The amount of open space in a compartment
The measure of water's flow through soil
The flow of liquid or gas through a barrier
Me

The soil, like my insides, has filled up.
The water overfills its underground banks.
It is bubbling up and back on itself and now.
Here we are, bending to the weight of another rain but still
buoyed by a certain knowing
—the kind that comes from experience
    that says this has to stop.
An unwiped windshield has the same obtuse
reinterpretation as my eyes do.
The same refraction that bends all the edges
and makes it okay to see through the tears.
I am open and drawn to you.

Epilogue
Your name

From the moment your name was yours, it fit. At once easy to picture and impossible to hold.

There is much to make of a river and how it helps us see, navigate, locate ourselves, and move through the world—both purposefully and uncontrollably. We—as a people—know these channels inside and out and yet they are mysterious. Outposts to civilizations have been built around them. They have been mapped and remapped by cartographers as the rivers themselves mapped their way through the landscape. They have been prayed to and prayed over, they have marked time in their bends and marked borders between lands—ones less arbitrary than the lines we draw over the maps. And importantly, rivers prove the wisdom of acceptance because in their nature is change.

You too do all of this. Your body was tiny but your presence is magnificent. Your time was short but your imprint is permanent. It is a now a mark from which we can start to recount time, like counting distance from the headwaters.

Before you were born, but after we knew you could not live, time was impossibly slow as the world around us seemed to stop. It was beautiful and heartbreaking to feel everything to my core, the way you do when time stops or a river is born. Then everything happened at once with doctors and research, morality and choices; a rush of ethical questions that tossed us and turned us inside out, the way I imagine any single droplet experiences a waterfall. And then you were born. An hour later you died, but somehow that doesn't seem to be the important thing because you keep on.

Like a river you will not run linearly. You will be more beautiful than a straight line and more fearless than order would allow. You will at times look still and calm, reflecting the clouds overhead given to each round edge. In this form, you are ready for a pebble to be tossed and a tear to drop in. We will watch the concentric circles ripple outward from there. A place for quiet investigation. Other times you will rip through us with force and chaos, you will be filled with the power of gravity and glaciers melting and time will disappear. We will be caught, submerged and tumbling, the way sand and shells are where the river is swallowed by the sea.

Because your name is River every rain is a visitation and every bridge is an invitation, which means around here, you are a ubiquitous mystery.